MARKERS

Two Friends Share Their History

Through Poetry

Dan K. Utley

&

Claire Martindale

STEPHEN F. AUSTIN STATE UNIVERSITY PRESS

Production Manager: Kimberly Verhines
Cover photos: Lee Russell
Book Design: Mallory LeCroy

IBSN: 978-1-62288-916-7

For more information: Stephen F. Austin State University Press
P.O. Box 13007 SFA Station
Nacogdoches, Texas 75962
sfapress@sfasu.edu
936-468-1078

Distributed by Texas A&M University Press Consortium
www.tamupress.com

*To my husband, Steve Martindale, and to the memory
of my parents, Harvey S. and Henrietta (Stilwell) Williams,
for their love and encouragement.*

—Claire

*To my wife, Debby, the first to inspire and then
to listen to the resulting words, and to my sister, Jane Utley, who helped
me see beyond the boundaries we build for ourselves.*

—Dan

CONTENTS

Three: Moving Shadows

Four: Reflections from Within

INTRODUCTION

This book is a reflection of a friendship that has continued strong for more than four decades. It began in October 1979 with the building of a team at the Texas Historical Commission (THC) in Austin. Claire Williams was then the Director of Research tasked with overseeing the state's impressive stock of historical markers. At the time, Texas had more markers—and some might argue more history—than any other state, and it has not relinquished that distinction in the intervening years. Currently, Texas boasts close to 20,000 official markers, with a couple of hundred more added each year.

To maintain the inventory of public history and to keep the momentum going, the new director—recently promoted from the position of marker writer—took a chance on a young schoolteacher (Dan Utley) who shared her passion for telling stories of the people's past. Together, the new Research Division team of director and marker writer (there was also an administrative assistant) worked with county historical commissions and THC commissioners to place markers all across the Lone Star State. Their jobs were to review marker applications to ensure accuracy, and then to draft inscriptions that, with quite limited text, would convey to the marker readers—students, heritage tourists, and history buffs alike—such concepts as context, significance, frame of reference, interpretation, and historical integrity. The topics were wide-ranging, reflecting the rich diversity of the state, and so the team members worked on subjects ranging from architecture to cemeteries and from military battles to women's clubs. And along the way, the two public historians became friends—lasting friends.

Given the personal preferences that shape careers and lifeways, the team parted ways in 1982, with each team member venturing out to explore new horizons and, in effect, new markers. Through the years and distance, though, the friendship continued, enriched by respect and pride, and enhanced by occasional visits, phone calls, cards and letters, and shared poetry. That brings the story full circle in a way for us, albeit with the abiding assurance that there will be more thoughts and memories to share with each other in the years ahead. Thanks for traveling with us on that journey.

Dan K. Utley, Pflugerville, Texas
Claire Martindale, Bridgewater, Virginia

I. SENSE OF PLACE

Creek crossing on the Ranch Road near Austin. *Courtesy Claire Martindale.*

RANCH ROAD

Your car knows every twist
and dip as this old road
plunges off the mesa toward the river.
High summer sun glints
off limestone and bakes the earth with white heat
as blinding as a snowfall.
Slow-roasting juniper and cactus scent the air,
but old landmarks have vanished.
No trace of the tank where rodeo
ponies came to drink.
Cattle guards disappeared
when the route was paved.
Middle-class dreams sprout
off the side roads now,
cradled in dark topsoil
where alien crepe myrtles take root.
The high-pitched hum of cicadas
drowns the swish of sprinklers
watering sidewalks.
At the lip of the mesa
you slow for a sharp bend
and your first glimpse of the river,
lazy, green, unchanging.

Claire Martindale

ACOMA PUEBLO, 1978

If I could drive one road again
it might be the one up to Sky City
where women shyly sold pots and
apple pies from rockbound homes
with screen doors barely opened
and their eyes quietly averted.
We were young then, though,
and always thought the road would
stay open, as it has for centuries, and
we would, no doubt, return someday
for another touch, another taste.

Dan K. Utley

SKYWARD

Wendell Berry just reminded me that
"Clouds are rarely absent from our sky,"
and that, in turn, recalled a time when,
for little apparent reason, we reclined
with dear friends in the cool grass of a
sloping summer lawn to gaze skyward,
focusing our shared visual energies on
isolated clouds to make them disappear.
As I remember now in my mind's sky,
it worked, as others said it would, and
we, with our backs to the earth, simply
changed the heavenly Texas skyscape
for one brief moment of one brief day.
I can only wonder if others noticed and
if we will ever have such grace again.

Dan K. Utley

TYLER ARCHIVES

Was he there in that historic photo
of young men and old cars in
front of the business school?
I couldn't tell across the years.
I wanted him to be;
I still want him to be.
I want to find him where
I've never seen him before,
and so I search.
For now, it's enough
to step outside the past
and see in the distance
the buildings he saw
when he was starting out.
Did he pause as I have?
Did he stop to remember?
Did he allow himself to think,
"I wonder if my son will
come here someday?"

I still *want* him to be

Dan K. Utley

ASPARAGUS

We signed the papers in December
and moved in New Year's Eve.
Spring in our new home
was a revelation.
Jonquils rose from dormant earth.
Pink and white peonies sprang
from the mulched slope.
Scraggly branches turned lavender
and smelled of lilac.

In mid-spring came the green
shoots beside the shed.
Ripe heads of tender asparagus
pushed aside the soil,
ready to be snapped
and steamed.

There was sustenance
for more than body
in those sprouts,
much more than seedlings
we planted ourselves.

This sustenance drew
on the mystery
of a Garden planted
by unseen hands.
Here was food
that required neither
foresight nor toil.

Every spring the patch
beside the shed
recalls that Garden.
We snap the tender spears
and taste of Eden.

Claire Martindale

RATCLIFF LAKE

If I must pay to enter the woods,
this is as good a place as any.
Folding money in a white envelope,
expecting no change in return—
Although, truth be told,
it's change I earnestly seek as I
drive on down the road.

Dan K. Utley

The refectory at Ratcliff Lake, built by the Civilian Conservation
Corps during the New Deal. *Courtesy Dan K. Utley.*

A Vermont whirligig at home in Texas. *Courtesy Dan K. Utley.*

WHIRLIGIG

Somewhere in Vermont I bought a whirligig
and brought it home on a plane stowed beneath
my seat, its jaybird wings cautiously akimbo.
It was the summer, and as countless summers go,
roadside memories have long since faded amid
fleeting landscapes of much younger journeys.
I think I found him, though, residing with avian
friends gathered to harness winds along the way.
His home was not that far from Old Bennington,
where I had earlier stopped at a quiet graveyard
to seek the tomb of Robert Frost, like countless
others have, as witnessed by the graveside trail,
and to wonder beneath the canopy of trees—
not yet yellowed—of a lover's quarrel with life.

Dan K. Utley

DON PEDRITO'S SHRINE

Bent by time, but buoyed by hope,
the old lady lifts the lichgate latch
and enters the quiet graveyard.
She doesn't pause to pay respects
but makes her way to the shrine,
where she kneels before a metal altar
and prays for her grandson, a marine.
She lights a candle and watches the fumes,
mingled with breath and faith, vent away.
She returns as she came, silent and slow,
relinquishing her place to a trucker,
who leaves his rig running on the road.
He's in a hurry, but foregoes haste for grace,
calling on the spirit of a *curandero* to
keep his family safe while he's away.
A young couple mingles in the store,
unsure of the herbs and packaged cures, but
embarrassed by shallow, stirring beliefs.
Relenting, they buy a candle and add to the pyre.
The curious tourist surveys it all and lingers
to view the *milagros*, the handwritten notes,
the faded photos, and the words of praise.
He studies the crutches in the corner,
remnants of miracles, stacked in mute testimony
to the inherent power of a sacred place.
Confused and cautious, he also lights a candle
and does his best with a silent prayer.
What could it hurt? At the very least
it's just another flame; at best it's not.
He feels a presence, perhaps his own,
and turns to be sure no one's there.
Returning to his car, he heads on down the road
and passes the trucker along the way,
honking as he does to acknowledge a brother.

Dan K. Utley

Don Pedrito prayer candle. *Courtesy Dan K. Utley.*

SOLSTICE

I watched the sun race
      across a December sky
            chasing a thin wisp of cloud
                    and catching it just at the
                              horizon

      like a match to cotton
      it set the cloud ablaze
flames of crimson and yellow flared on either side

naked branches stretched their spindly fingers
      toward the warmth
the glow struck a shallow pond and set it
                   glistening
                     with white fire

the moon turned its face
      to glimpse the display
but the sun had vanished

only its embers lingered
      a thin line of red-gold
            cooling to the warm gray of ash,
                leaving me to face the cold blackness of the
                            long night.

Claire Martindale

ON THE PERE MARQUETTE

A thin gray scrim of fog with a light brocade of mist
marked the Michigan morning as two friends eased
the dark green Old Towne in the softly-swirling,
coffee-colored waters of PM's Gleason Landing.
just around the first bend—or a bend or two past that—
a gangly, unshaven, toothless sentinel clad in yellow
guarded the passage, and the common cultural thread
of words from stream to shore and back were of fish.
"Seen any yet?"
"Sure. A few."
"How come they're not on the shore with you then?"
A grin, a friendly mumbled line, and understanding.
And the dark green Old Towne eased silently by to
the next bend, the next scene, the next chance to cast.
It may have been like this for generations, who knows?
Each bend brings promise, a new deep pool to plumb,
and new shared stories—linear conversations offered
in circular fashion along a gently meandering stream,
on down the way to Bowman's Bridge—and beyond.

Dan K. Utley

LAKESIDE SHADOWS

Dad and I stood near here,
together,
decades ago,
sometime before I realized
he had been a boy
and I would be a man.
Back then it was enough
to skip stones and whittle,
and row out far from shore.
I'm older now than my
dad was then, and older
than he would ever be,
so I return, alone.
Waves have come and gone
since then, but the scent of
pines that shaded us that day
remains and enfolds.
High branches cast down
welcoming shadows,
deep and memorable, like
a troupe of dancing ghosts
that has long since danced away.

Dan K. Utley

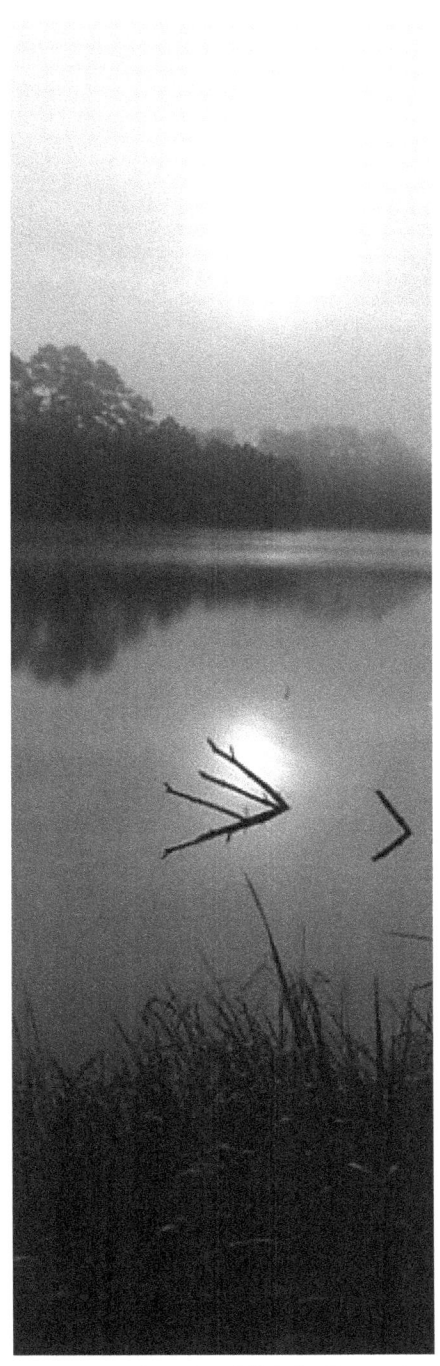

Early morning, Ratcliff Lake Recreation
Area, Davy Crockett National Forest
near Ratcliff, Texas. *Courtesy Dan K. Utley.*

TRANSIT

Meridian, Mississippi, 2 a.m.
Just a day off the plane
you stare with new eyes
at the harsh lights of the interstate.
"This is the poorest state
in the country," you say,
"with six lanes lit up like noontime.
Zambia has no highway like this,
even in Lusaka."

Later, you sleep while I drive.
You dream of African roads,
narrow and dark.
I tune in a country station on the radio
and steady the car
against the roar of 18-wheelers
hurrying to fill our emptiness.

Claire Martindale

SITTING IN THE BIG WOODEN TENT

Thank goodness there are days predestined for thinking,
when deep rest and reflection are more or less required.
otherwise, we might have worked on contracts or research,
shaped glass and mixed grout, or fretted about deadlines.
Instead, arriving early for a Chautauquan event on a cool
and crisp summer morning (so unlike our home in Texas),
we sat and thought about the upcoming talk, but also of
upcoming opportunities, like supervising student teachers
or taking part in a children's hospital mosaic for Debby, or
starting a new semester and finishing book projects for me.
Who knew that before the day was out we would be buying
sweaters for comfort, or that the next day we would drench
ourselves in Niagara's spray or take a hike into Canada?
We now see that predestination has its place, and that it
looks much like a wooden bench in western New York.

Dan K. Utley

KING STREET

One bright Charleston summer day,
a stranger stopped to let me know,
"People who live here walk
on the shady side of the street."
With that, he tipped his hat, grinned,
and continued on his way up King.

I might have figured it out alone,
certainly by my second shirt that day.
Or maybe it would have come as the
sky faded softly in a broken breeze
and I strolled arm in arm with my wife.

I recalled the words today, decades later,
and smiled in the shadows of old facades,
reflecting on a time when a stranger
crossed the street just to let me know.

Dan K. Utley

Pews in the Chautauqua Amphitheatre, Chautauqua,
New York, 2012. *Courtesy Dan K. Utley.*

BERMUDA

From the top of Gibbs Hill Lighthouse, you can see
the entirety of the archipelago, and you wonder how
Bermuda escapes being swamped by the sea. Over a
thousand miles to the north, nothing but the vast Atlantic
stretches between you and the shores of Nova Scotia.
Due west, 600 miles away, lies the closest landmass,
the shipwreck coast of Carolina. And yet 400 years ago
this impossibly small patch of land and reefs was site of
a drama that bolstered the failing English colony of Virginia.

It was northeast of the lighthouse, near the beach at
Fort St. Catherine, where the shipping channel zigzags
around the reefs. Here came the great *Sea Venture*,
a sailing ship sent in 1609 to rescue the foundering
few left in Jamestown. Blown off course by hurricane
winds, it wrecked on the reefs within sight of Bermuda.
The survivors fashioned two ships from the *Sea Venture's*
frame and Bermuda cedar. Many months later they
arrived on Virginia's shores to encourage the settlers
until another supply convoy brought rescue.

At Gibbs Hill Lighthouse, you gaze at almost 200 small
islands sprinkled atop the waves—Bermuda. What were
the odds that *Sea Venture* would find this slip of land
out of the hurricane's fury? That all aboard would survive
the wreck? That the land would sustain them and help feed
Jamestown's hungry? What prayers were spoken and answered
here in the middle of the deep, here in Bermuda?

Claire Martindale

EVEN IN WOODVILLE

Even in Woodville,
as I hear pine-filtered whispers of wind
over darkling shadows of Turkey Creek
and follow red dirt trails,
ancient, imagined, recalled,
across places redrawn by time,
even then—
and maybe even then the most—
I yet long for Woodville.

Dan K. Utley

T & N O DEPOT
WOODVILLE, TEXAS

The Texas and New Orleans depot, Woodville,
Texas, 1938. *Courtesy Dan K. Utley.*

MILLENIAL CREEK

Bright reflections dance at the water's edge with
shadows in dappled light along a nameless stream;
mosaics of the moment amid glimpses of the past.
As time-worn tesserae gathered by the artist in a
crowded city, on a country road, around a square,
or along a yellowed trail in a highland wood,
and reconfigured with unmistakable purpose.
Fleeting scenes that mark the days, like the
soulful sound of a friend's lament, spoken thoughts
and midnight laughter, or the gathering of familiar
spirits to scan the skies and watch the pages turn.
New horizons, new companions, and newly
fashioned plans for the hopes that lie ahead.
And so the water flows.

Dan K. Utley

IMMERSION

I dip into the waters of the Congo.
Tannin from floating leaves stains it as dark as oolong
and the equator sun turns it just as warm.

When water pressure in the guest house drops,
we don swimsuits and carry our soap
to the banks of the Congo.

We lather and rinse
as narrow pirogues float perilously close,
hugging the shore to escape the current at midstream.

Families on the way to market,
fishermen returning with a catch,
they gape at the pale intruders sharing their waters.

The Congo for them is a highway,
reservoir of food,
home to those who live on their boats.

Far across the water
we see a fringe of trees.
Only an island, we're told.

The opposite shore lies beyond that,
and our world
farther still.

Claire Martindale

Pirogues on the Congo River. *Courtesy Claire Martindale.*

BROWNWOOD

When I worked for the state,
historian without portfolio, it seemed,
I drove the roads alone many times—
blue ones, black ones, dotted, and dirt.
Through every county I passed towns
that were, that are, and that might be,
and each one had a name as I recall.
I walked the lonely rural graveyards
and recorded standing chimneys,
ranch gates, burr burners, pony trusses,
and crumbling schools filled with hay.
On midnight walks round silent squares
there were gaps and ghost signs, and
hollow theaters that once thrummed
with lights that welcomed all, separately.
When I venture there again, I remember.
My stories are scattered everywhere,
like when I sat in an Abilene diner
mentally retracing my route to Austin and
realizing I was in Brownwood instead,
eighty miles to the good.

Dan K. Utley

II. ENCOUNTERS

SPIRIT AT THE BACKDOOR

—for Mabel Prater Utley

Late in the night an unsure knock
came from the backdoor as we
gathered to clear the kitchen
from the evening's simple meal.
The voice, unsure and hoarse,
but somehow resolute, drifted
alone through the open screen
like a stage-borne spirit from
beyond a darkened scrim that
hides an actor's face from view
but never belies his presence.
"Please, ma'am. Some food?
I just need something to eat."
"You stay there," she replied,
"and I'll fix you something."
And from the still-warm stove
she filled a plate with beans,
crowned it with a square of
yellow cornbread, and passed
it beyond the screen door to the
outstretched hand from a man,
still offstage and never fully seen.
"God bless you, ma'am," the spirit
said, and "You as well," the reply.
Closely, as through a window, I
watched his back on the stoop,
as he ate and then drifted away
in the stillness of a Lufkin night.

Dan K. Utley

SHE WAS WALKING

Windshield wipers flicking at high speed
gave me a glimpse of her through
sheets of blowing rain. She was walking
along a street near my house, her umbrella
a useless encumbrance in the downpour.

I turned my car in her direction,
not the direction I intended to go.
Something compelled me to stop.
Some force forbade me to drive on
and watch her mirrored image struggle
against the storm. Her maid's uniform,
the color of her skin, told me she did
not live in this neighborhood. When
I stopped, something in turn compelled
her to accept the ride. This was not the
usual practice for either of us—giving
and receiving rides with strangers.

She slid in, wary, solemn, unsure of this
Samaritan. In as few words as necessary,
she directed me to the bus stop, a short
drive away. Nothing more was uttered,
except "Thank you" and "You're welcome"
when we reached that destination.

I glanced in the mirror to see her gain
the shelter of the covered stop,
then turned back the way I came.
We were two travelers along the road
on a rain swept afternoon. For a few
brief moments, we rode together.

Claire Martindale

BAJA LAJITAS

Summoned by our shouts and waves,
two men dragged a metal boat
from the mesquite-shrouded ramada,
pushed off into the Rio Grande,
and rowed our way.
As they cut upstream to work the drift,
we said our goodbyes.
We were friends for one day only,
and her name is long forgotten,
but I remember the stories she shared
about history along the Big Bend.
She had come from Mexico and was
headed back to her adobe home.
It was sunset as she seated herself
in the boat, stowed her satchel, and waved.
Without talking, we listened, first to the
cadence of creaking oarlocks and then
the muffled roar of the engine as her truck
climbed sand hills up and out of the valley.
The ramada men resumed their shaded rest
and we sat in waning sunlight across the river
taking in the tapestry—
not hurried to end the day.
Only the river moved, it seemed.
Only the river moved.

"We better go," Curtis finally said,
reaching out to touch my shoulder.

Back at Ivy's cantina we sat and watched
two old dogs with bandana collars
play in courtyard dust outside the pen
of the beer-drinking goat, Clay Henry.

Dan K. Utley

MAIDEN AUNTS

You might suppose
that my grandmother's sisters
were both old maids,
but Hazel was married
and widowed young.
Eula Mae never wed the man
in the faded snapshot.
They said he did her wrong.
She had a spinster's
name, but a ready wit.

We called them Hay and Boo,
when they lived together
in their later years.
Their names sounded
like a vaudeville team,
and they bantered like troupers.

Their visits were filled
with tales of the slow children
they taught
and quips about dismal football
played at their alma mater.
They bestowed most
of the family nicknames
that stuck.

They took their mother
and sister to Mexico,
four old ladies
at Xochimilco, flirting
with the Indian boatman
and laughing.

Claire Martindale

The Weatherly women visit the Floating Gardens of Xochimilco near Mexico City, c. late 1940s. *Courtesy Claire Martindale*

MR. CHARLIE

When we played Magnolia Hills
he would draw his true wood driver
from his moth-eaten bag and
approach the tee box with the quiet
determination of his military years.
Taking measured stock of the terrain
through squinted eyes,
he would draw back and fire
with all his aging body had to give,
scattering his plastic pocket protector—
pens, glasses, and cigarettes—
several yards ahead.
He always gave it all he had,
even when his aged irons shattered
or he hit a deer in the head.
We kept score in balls lost and found
amid tight fairways in deep woods,
where we counted snakes as hazards.
And at least once each round,
for reasons known best to him,
but maybe just for grins,
Mr. Charlie would stop, growl,
and bark like a dog.
                    Dan K. Utley

3:42 A.M.

I sit to document that it's 3:42
on a Friday morning
and I can't sleep,
my mind dancing and darting,
while those who set it in motion,
without even knowing my name,
sleep my rightful sleep.
I envy them at this small hour,
and yet I would not go without care,
and I would not shy from change.
Life goes on in the margins
even as I wrestle with the day.
They will always be, I know,
and so will I—
restless and sleepless,
awaiting four bells tolling
in the deepness of the night.
                    Dan K. Utley

Charles F. Blanks (aka Mr. Charlie) with his wife, Marjorie, c. 1980s.
Courtesy Charles F. Blanks, Jr.

LE POMPIER

"Un pompier," the teenager
responded to my question,
asked in French. My friends were
hosting Jean-Luc, a high school
foreign exchange student.
His English was pretty good;
they spoke tourist French.
They invited me one night
for dinner and conversation.

French classes in college
left me with passable
pronunciation—all those nasal
sounds, and the rolling "r".
With knowing how to ask
"where is the bathroom" and
"how much does this cost"
and decipher the rapid response
of a native speaker.

In any study of language there
are words that stick in your brain,
having nothing to do with directions
or buying souvenirs. Words like
"le fauteuil" or "rez-de-chausee."
Or that marvelous French idiom
for "window shopping." It's just
serendipity that files those
meanings in your memory.

That was the case when my friends
said, "We asked what work his father
does but couldn't understand
Jean-Luc's answer." So I asked their
question and laughed out loud
when the young man answered.

It was one of those words!
"Un pompier," Jean-Luc said.
His father was a fireman.

Claire Martindale

TRACTOR ON THE WHEELOCK ROAD

Years ago, on a backroad near the backwoods town of Wheelock,
I rounded an inside curve and came up behind an old John Deere
puttering slowly along from field to field as if in survival mode.
Not an uncommon scene in rural Texas, where backroads are
often farm to markets, but what caught my attention that
autumn eve as shadows lengthened were its two drivers.
The chief pilot, it seemed, was a little boy, maybe eight or nine,
and as he gripped the oversized steering wheel, he stared down
the road with great intensity, albeit it in a good-natured manner.
He was focused, with immediate purpose and maybe a bit of fear.
On the tongue back behind him, amid the fenders and singing tires
stood an older gentleman who appeared to be the seasoned pro,
comfortable yet obviously cautious in his precarious stance, and
wearing faded denim overhauls, a straw hat, and blue plaid shirt.
I followed carefully, unnoticed at first, but respectful of the team.
As the curve played out to a straighter path, I eased my pickup
carefully around the pair and on down the backroad to the east.
As I passed, as if in slow motion, the old farmer turned my way
and caught my eye, grinning widely as he did. In his smile and
wave and warm regard, I clearly caught what his heart conveyed:
"Fellow traveler, this is my grandson, in whom I am well pleased."

Dan K. Utley

MEZZALUNA

Stratified perspectives on a November night,
with layers and streams outlined in yellow;
frames of reference framed referentially.
'Will my son be okay?"
'What's the meaning of friends?"
"Is there life post-present?"
Too few answers to too many questions,
but the seekers are not deterred.
Maybe they'll find it in O'Keeffe's spirit,
dancing on a well-worn page,
or maybe in the tranquility
of lifetime lessons learned and shared.
The existential journey of thoughts,
after all, brings souls together
without the bounds of time,
and therein lies the truth
that makes it all worthwhile.

Dan K. Utley

THE SENTINEL'S SHADOW

Narcissus dancing at the river bridge.
"I am the gateway.
Come see the gateway.
Rush through the gateway."
Where is the soldier tonight?
Has he forsaken his post for a
shimmering shadow, the moonlit
reflection at the riverbend edge?
Go cast your lot with the sentinel.
He's lost, but seek his shadow
and study the margins—
linger in the margins
and redefine the past.
Choose what you will of life,
but cling to the cliffs.
Search for meaning in the margin
of the sentinel's shadow.
Taunt the rain and follow the moon.

Dan K. Utley

JUBILEE

There seemed to be flowers everywhere . . .
Gladiolas decorating the old Oak Grove Church
        and filling the arms of bridesmaids.
A sweet-scented gardenia on the bride's Bible.
In the midst of the flowers they stood,
        in a white satin gown and a black tuxedo.
The bride's father spoke the vows,
        and bride and groom repeated them—nervously, solemnly.

There have been flowers ever since . . .
Birthday flowers, Valentine bouquets, a rose to say I'm sorry.
Flowers in the garden of a home lovingly tended.

There have been solemn moments, too,
        and nervous ones.
But also hours of joy, contentment, sweet togetherness.
Moments to celebrate the birth of three children—
        to take pride in each of their lives.
Moments to mourn family members, loved and gone.

There are the vows,
spoken with love,
and honored through all these years.

At the center of life, there is still the Bible,
        and the Scripture's ageless declaration on love.
Love, it says, is patient
                and hopeful
                        and confident.
Loves never bullies or broods.
Above all, love endures.

They tested those words,
        and found them true.
They found that love, in the end,
                not only endures,
                        but triumphs.

And so, after fifty summers, fifty winters,
fifty autumns and springs,
50 times 50 times 50 I-love-you's spoken,
we are back at Oak Grove Church with flowers, friends, family
and a moment that is not solemn at all!

Their love calls us here today for jubilee.
We celebrate together—
              a church filled with flowers,
                    and two lives lived with love.
Claire Martindale

THE IVANHOE PINE

Together, they made their way along the high sand ridge
above the lake, amid blackjack oaks and bluestem grasses.
On a slope by a yaupon thicket they found the longleaf pine
that would mark their first Christmas as husband and wife.
It was young, as they were, and its scant limbs were more
than enough for the limited ornaments they had acquired.
It seemed at home in their small cabin, with decorations of
Spanish moss, glittered pinecones, and sweet gum balls.
There have been many since then, each with its own place
in the accumulated past of thirty years together, but none
that comes so quickly to mind, as the scent of pine, mixed
with crisp December air, speaks to the soul of love and
hope and promise—the gifts of the holiday season—and
the couple walks again in memories of the Ivanhoe woods.
Dan K. Utley

INVINCIBLE AT THE MILL*

The old bell rings at the sawmill church,
blocked from the highway and houses
by storied stacks of fresh-cut lumber
drying in the summer's morning sun.
At first there's no response, but then
the presence of distant rolling thunder
pushing ahead of it sounds of laughter.

Bare black feet on yellow pine boards
make them clap in a percussive rhythm
to a ground beat of place and purpose,
as the children leap from stack to stack.
To most there's no hesitation, but some
pause and plan and then miss the mark,
skittering down the sides to start again.

As they near the church, the children
alight and stroll reverently to the door,
where the Invincible gives each a hug
and tells them how glad she is they came.
As echoes of thunder roll past the church,
the scent of dusty music fills the yard
and flattened notes from a time-worn piano
strain for recognition of past tuned glories.

Children stand on pews and clap their hands
as a girl fingers keys once robed in ivory
and leads the rest in *Jesus Loves Me*.
These are Baptist kids in a Baptist mill,
Where a bunkered church means hope,
except, as some might say, on Saturdays,
when older folks worship elsewhere
under neon clouds and jukebox promise.

But this is Monday, and while they return
to dog the logs and stack new boards,
their kids listen to summer's missionary
tell of places and ideas far removed from
the company hill above Big Turkey Creek.

They sing and play and recite and make
plaster casts of praying hands—their own.

At the end of the week, their pastor will
beckon them back at night, as families.
Together, they'll sing hymns of praise,
survey the brightly colored artwork,
and see a play of the Good Samaritan.
As the sun descends below pine-clad hills,
they'll slowly file out, stopping at the door
to offer thanks to the Invincible, Miss Jane.

They'll talk of blessings, decisions, and faith,
and their voices will mingle with the crickets
as they meander back among the stacks.
No thunder that night—just quiet, clear skies.
In the darkness of the silent mill, we'll follow.
I'll hold her hand in mine as we walk to the road,
and I whisper, "Good job, Sis. Let's head home."

Dan K. Utley

*Invincibles were young people who served as summer missionaries under the sponsorship of the Baptist General Convention of Texas. My sister, Jane Utley, led vacation Bible Schools in the rural sawmill communities of Tyler County in the summer of 1964.

Jane Utley, lower right, with the summer Bible school class of a rural church near Woodville, Texas, 1960s. *Courtesy Dan K. Utley.*

AULD LANG SYNE

Dateless on New Year's Eve,
three girlfriends made a party
around the coffee table.
The blender was their bartender—
fruity, frozen rum
to celebrate being young.

Sitting cross-legged on the rug,
they leaned close
to share their secrets—
the hell of bad bosses,
the giddy thrill of new romance.

At midnight, they contrived
to predict each other's futures,
soothsayers spinning benevolent
fortunes for beloved friends.

Ignorant of the subtler tricks of life,
their vision soared no farther
than the clock ticking
toward tomorrow's dawn.

All they knew of the future
was the joy of together—
of now.

Claire Martindale

THE CONCERT

Sister planned the trip,
bought the tickets,
persuaded Brother to drive
us two hours to Houston.
We dressed up—skirts
and nylon stockings. No
jeans at concerts then.

No reserved seats either.
We lined up early outside
the auditorium, unshaded
from the August midday
heat. When teenage
girls began fainting,
the doors were opened.

We claimed two seats
and waited for hours,
eyeing the stage. Who
remembered the opening
act? Who cared? Occasional
shrieks marked imagined
sightings until, at last, chaos.
They were really there.

When the first note sounded,
no one could hear it,
nor any of the notes
that came afterward.
Only the screams, the shrieks,
the uncontrolled emotion.

Somehow we knew the
words we couldn't hear and
sang along to music
obliterated by squalling fans.
Sister pressed her lips
to my ear to name songs
I couldn't recognize.
Bass notes thrummed up through

the floor. How did the players
hear each other, I wondered.

Brother picked us up after
spending his day at the beach,
and we floated home. My ears
buzzed and ached for two days.
I tucked away my ticket stub,
still safe after half a century.
In 1965 we paid five dollars for
a Beatles concert and owned
an unmatched adventure.

Claire Martindale

HARBINGER

I've got nothing against the jay.
In fact, I have a painting of one
on a library wall and a ceramic
one or two on shelves nearby.
Males and females alike are true
blue and marvelously detailed,
their flash of splendid colors
always a showy welcome along
a deep and darkened woodland
trail where shadows starken in
the changing lights of the day.
Unlike the harbinger jay, though,
I feel no need, upon its arrival,
to hasten my stride and plunge
on ahead, announcing to no one
in particular, "A bird is coming!"

Dan K. Utley

Ceramic blue jays on a cloudy day.
Courtesy Dan K. Utley.

eliza honey bishop

Wiry, witty, and lovably stubborn,
she was the lower-case doyenne
of pine-clad Houston County, and
to all, its designated historian.
The past was hers to know and
hers to tell, and even hers to keep;
few dared challenge her take on life.
Firing from a manual typewriter that
served her well as a rural stringer,
she launched countless volumes of
stories, opinion pieces, and letters,
never shying in the shadows or
taking backroad routes to truth.
"History happened here," she told,
and "here" was any tract of land
sufficient for a roadside marker.
Bridging the generation gaps, she
brought the past to the present,
leaving the rest to those who
would move it ever forward with
new layers and new perspectives,
and then she joined the ranks of
those she gave a life to remember.

Dan K. Utley

DOWN HOME

As I read the menu
of the Down Home Café.
the waitress asked,
"Has anybody ever told you
That you look like Ted Kennedy?"
"He's dead, you know."
"Yeah," she said, "I know."
"I'll have the roast beef."

Dan K. Utley

THE REUNION

Over onion dip
I face a stranger
I haven't seen in forty years.

I start to speak my name,
but she knows me, she says,
not as the scabby-kneed child I was then.
She sees another, gone long ago.
"You look like your mother," she says,
remembering a face, and a friend,
she knew as an awkward teenager.

Her gaze moves beyond
the cheese and crackers
to a past she loved enough
to join in reunion.
Her memories take flesh
in my aging face.

I also came seeking
a glimpse of history shared.
Now I need only turn to the mirror.
Claire Martindale

FIFTY FOR FIFTY

Twenty years ago I sat alone
In a pine-laden park,
now burned over and bare, and
contemplated old paths to a new age.
Pay more attention, I wrote,
to the magical world around me,
and I was sincere—and then older.
Packing my thoughts quietly, closely,
I first saw her just beyond my margin,
magical, certainly, and cautiously still.
Tan with thoughtful, languid eyes,
she studied me—and I her in return.
Here was the challenge of the day
and a new half century.
I was in her home, after all, and
she in my promising prayer;
a lingering doe and a reverent man,
in a pine-laden park,
now burned over and bare.
Dan K. Utley

A trail through a burned over section of Bastrop State Park
Courtesy Dan K. Utley

PRAIRIE DANCER

As I dropped out of the Guadalupes
headed south on 54,
it first appeared off to my left,
bouncing down a wide arroyo.
At first no more than a novelty,
it became, with time, a companion
on the open stretch of lonely road
north of Sulphur Creek.

In tandem, we passed the muted miles,
sharing an open landscape
without challenge or concern.
I marveled at its character,
tenuous yet resolute, as it
danced along the broken desert floor,
an ephemeral sprite of wind and dust.

What if we were to meet, I thought?
And with that, as on cue, the whirlwind
turned my way, and I knew it to be.
I steadied myself for the encounter,
unsure of what it might entail, but
eager to know the answer.

Somewhere north of the bridge,
the prairie dancer left the stage,
brushed me broadside with
graceful power and then ascended
while I smiled, sighed, adjusted
my rearview mirror, and headed
on down to Van Horn.

Dan K. Utley

MILES

I knew it long before I heard it,
But when I did, it was far beyond
What I thought I understood.

Air from somewhere deep inside
Rippled over unseen shoals,
And blew sweet and light—
            and blue.

And my soul rested.
It simply walked away and rested,
            as I somehow knew it would,
Long before I heard it,
And long before I understood.

Dan K. Utley

CRUSTACEANS

7 or 8 stand together
but apart
in morning's light,
wearing self-consciousness
like bivalve shells,
their elbows tucked
tight as if
the merest touch
threatened
contamination.
Even their eyes dare
not stray beyond
hooded flickers
seeking a glimpse
of the yellow bus.
When they were younger
this morning wait
was filled with giggling
and poking.
Now bodies changing
and armor hardening,
they draw within
the safety
of separate selves.

Claire Martindale

ORION

When the stars of Orion sail toward midnight,
I remember my grandfather.

A farm boy who earned the title doctor,
teacher, principal, college president.
He lobbied senators, and, when he died,
The governor sent a telegram.

My memories are of different things.
He ate sardines on saltine crackers.
He sent me a bird's nest in the mail,
      the twigs and daubings carefully wrapped in newspaper.
For bedtime stories,
      he told about Natty Bumppo and Hans Brinker.
He spun tales of Greek mythology,
and showed me heroes and gods
      hiding in the twinkling constellations.

History books recount my grandfather's life.
Streets and buildings bear his name.
But I remember him best
when Orion, the Hunter,
      chases through the night sky.

Claire Martindale

BROTHERS ON A BRAIDED TRAIL

—for Curtis D. Tunnell, mentor and friend

One came to the plains in the shadow of the hawk,
picking cotton, tending mail, making red top stew.
He rested in the shade of broken Caprock canyons
and learned about people, both ancient and recent,
from the virtual yardstick of life's existence and a
common cultural rhythm of searches and dreams.

Years later in the Piney Woods, the other started
his journey, learning history from his father's stories
and watching hollow traditions fade in dappled light.
At home in the woods, alone in the city, drawn by
strains of the Old South, he headed west, while the
other made a long circle journey back home to Texas.

Somewhere in between, at the end of a decade, the
sojourners crossed paths, not knowingly at first,
but then in celebration of shared perspectives as
mainstream answers ill fit the questions, and rights
and wrongs reversed themselves on battlefields,
in ghettos, and along routes that strangers laid out.

It was perhaps only natural the two Texas travelers
would somehow come together to share stories,
to seek out new vistas, and to understand more of life.
With one purpose, many viewpoints, and much humor
they listened, learned, and lingered along a common trail,
Recording pockets of the past, even ones masquerading
as the present, and preserving for collective memory the
summary statements of bounteous and elusive parts.

What brought them together was a sense of place,
but not the kind packaged by planners and offered
to tourists in uniformed stations along the highways.
There was, in both travelers, an innate understanding
that history and life are where you found yourself,
and both often found themselves on the blue roads,
searching backdoors of history, where words, like
actions and memories, lingered for others to know.

There were East Texas peckerwoods and moss-draped graveyards, the Rio Grande, onion pickers, *curanderos*, reprobates, shade trees, treeless plains, dust storms, torrential rains, stonecarver mysteries, lichens and moss, fiddle music, yellow bandanas, pearly rainbows and sunsets, half-melted adobe churches, blackberry sellers, barbecue, abandoned schools, hillside arenas, grave toys, open mines, the scent of yucca, and the welcome shelter of chaparral.

Landscapes defining memories—some shared, some recalled, and some lost—only to return one day with a word and a grin. All are landmarks on a braided trail, signs for no one other than the travelers, who stay true to the course, content that the route remains unknown and without direction. It is enough for both that the traces are still there for reflection as the seasons change.

Dan K. Utley

"A Trail of Social Distance"
Pre-COVID trail sign. *Courtesy Dan K. Utley.*

A TRAIL OF SOCIAL DISTANCE
—In the time of pandemic

Each plant of the walking stick
breaks the silence as a ragged
cadence to unsure feet.
A lengthening distant shadow
determines the course for now,
and with eyes cast downward,
I seek mercy on the trail.
Will this be the stranger
whose breath will do me in?
Do I dare to stay the line,
or yield with distance for
one more chance alone?
Uncertain, I step aside and
stand motionless, reverent.
Casting a passing glance
into eyes as vague as mine,
I nod a voiceless greeting,
returned in kind, and brace
for the next encounter.

Dan K. Utley

AT THE FUNERAL

The three of us left
work that afternoon
and drove across town
to the A.M.E. Church.
Our friend, our coworker,
Lilly Mae, had lost her brother.
We dressed up to show
our respect and headed
to his funeral.
There weren't many seats
left in the little church,
but we found three together
near the back. As I looked
around at the mourners,

one thing surprised me most.
We were the only white
people there.
Lilly Mae's brother lived
in that little town his whole
life. He had worked with
and for white people. We all
shopped at the same Piggly-
Wiggly. We all ate fast
food from the same Hardees.
But with death came the old
divides. He was buried
in the black cemetery and
three friends of his sister
were the only white people
in attendance.
We drove back to work,
pondering the mysteries
of life and death, pondering,
too, the things that separate
us from neighbors who share
the same space and breathe
the same air.

Claire Martindale

OF TIME AND A PROMISE

I stopped in Caldwell for a kolache and coffee
to open my mind for an unfurling day.
I was off to give a talk that would mark
my last before retirement at week's end.

I wasn't sure of his path that morning,
but I saw stories that danced in his eyes,
yellowed with age in a friendly face—
a friendly, ebony, roadmap face—
and so I stayed to welcome
where the turns might take us out
beyond the gold Formica booths.

Hardscrabble truths rounded by time
and cloudless, boundless respect of
two old men sharing pasts in an
unrehearsed chance encounter
at the start of an otherwise routine day.

Yielding to time and a promise, I left,
reverently replaying a moment deferred.
A collector of recorded memoirs, I travel still,
in a world of context and shared authority.
But in a roadside bakery at winter's daybreak
I simply, without reason, let one get away.

I should have at least paid for his coffee.

Dan K. Utley

III. MOVING SHADOWS

BLACK GRANITE

One young man's name was Pete Winter,
someone I saw but never really knew
in my childhood. My mind's eye recalls
only vague perspectives, but I remember
laughter and fear as a soldier departed
From the Piney Woods of East Texas.

I run my hand along the lines of his name
not understanding why he had to die.
He's there with others for others to see,
and maybe there's truth in deep reflection.

The other one's name was Emmitt Till,
someone I never met but knew in books.
The visions in my mind's eye are very clear.
His crime was speaking to a white woman
and the sentence carried out was death
in the Piney Woods of Mississippi.

I run my hand along the lines of his name
Not understanding why he had to die.
He's there with others for others to see,
and maybe there's hope in streaming water.

Dan K. Utley

RETURNS

The doubts, as well as the hopes,
faded by three in the morning,
and I went off to bed,
pausing only to wake her and apologize
for the loss of dreams.
"How can that be?"
"Who are we now?"
I kissed her cheek in silent reply.
I had no answer then or later
when I aired my tires and
cycled out into a light and steady rain,
hoping I was somehow wrong
and showers would absolve.
Yet, five miles in on a seven-mile run,
I entered the open garage
of an empty house and cried.
I sat on the concrete floor and cried.

Dan K. Utley

1918

He rode the train to an army
post in the next state. My father's
older cousin, Sinclair. Volunteered
with the YMCA to support the soldiers.
Like so many, he couldn't help
even himself when Influenza
came to the camp. They brought
his body back on the train for his
young widow to bury.

She was a schoolteacher, my
grandfather's younger sister,
Mae Oma. The old snapshot shows
her with my mother and uncle
when they were babies. Where did
she catch the Flu? No one knows,
but it killed her just the same.

When finally it faded, that
generation didn't want to talk
about the Flu. As if naming the
pestilence would conjure it again.
As if remembering would keep pain
boiling like a kettle on the stove.

But our family told the next
generation. And spoke about Herbert,
the doughboy who was our great-uncle,
killed in France that same frightful
fall of 1918. How did they survive
their heartache, we wonder. And
wonder if we can do the same.
They speak to us still. Sinclair,
Mae Oma, Herbert. And all the
others. Whenever their story is told.
"Don't forget," they say.

"Don't forget."

Claire Martindale

In a scene hauntingly familiar today, public service workers
in 1918 donned masks to stop the spread of a pandemic.
Courtesy Wikimedia, public domain.

DEBBY, DAY 29
—in the time of pandemic

With tears in her eyes, she said,
"When this is over, I want to live."
And I knew.
But knowing is not an answer,
and distant dreams are hollow,
so she stands apart
and I cannot reach her sorrow.
Afraid and unsure,
she plans only for the day to come.
                    Dan K. Utley

IN LINE ON ELECTION DAY, GEORGIA 1988

Most of you could have voted for George Washington, you know.
Or someone like you,
            a man . . . a white man . . . a man with property.
But the rest of us
            wouldn't—couldn't—have stood with you then.
We joined this line later in our country's lifetime.

The old black man who lives in that tiny apartment
            beside the pizza place—
How long did Jim Crow hold the ballot just out of his reach?
He leans heavily on his walker, but his hand is strong as he pulls the lever.
He waited too long to be turned back by a little rheumatism.

There is the clerk from the convenience store.
Every election day her grandmother reminds her.
Granny was just a child when she witnessed
            her own mother make a mark on a ballot—
                    the first woman in their town, ever, to vote.
Today the clerk has her six-year-old daughter with her.
Granny said she should come.

Suffrage.
It's our right.
But the word whispers of the struggle and hardship that make it our duty,
too, even when the mayor is running unopposed.
                    Claire Martindale

OLD HANDS

They aren't shaped the way
they were years ago,
and they sometimes tremble
and often ache, but
they are warm, most days,
and fit together well enough
for a sense of love and
memories of the past,
when youthful hands
were of little concern.

Dan K. Utley

WATERCOURSE YEARS

I have heard them all before,
bound by the fog of myth,
the oft-told stories we all
recall and all repeat in the
watercourse years of youth—
the unchallenged times in
the winding years to now.
Yet, told with new voices
against a backdrop of time,
they resonate and renew as
though never heard before.
Words are replaced in kind
by streaming layers of love,
and I at once rest peacefully
in comforting silent shade of
new and relevant contexts I
never knew to unpack before.
My abiding question then is,
had I but lingered to listen in
The fog of long ago, would I be
farther down the watercourse,
or was the staging as it must
have been to get me here to
this reflective point in time?

Dan K. Utley

Dan Utley with his dad, Festus Utley, along the banks of Salado Creek near the historic Utley family homestead, Bell County, Texas, c. 1953. *Courtesy Dan K. Utley.*

DISADVANTAGED

The few years of his life had been pampered—
an oversized house on a private street
Private schools
Private clubs
Even a church where everyone else looked like
       his father, mother, brother, sister.

Now he and the other teenagers were far from their suburban Eden
in a part of town they'd never seen.
Wearing brand new work gloves and tool belts,
they tore rotted wood from a rickety porch,
       opened cans of paint to transform the weathered siding.

Looking down the row of houses so close they almost touched,
he saw behind each one an unfamiliar shape
a construction of wood and wire so alien
       it might have come from another world.
And, in truth, it did not come from his world.
A clothesline.

When told what it was, he opened his mouth
and asked the other question
      that revealed his poverty—
          "How does it dry the clothes?"

In a world where every space he inhabited
      was artificially cooled, heated, filtered,
the sun was reserved for resort islands
and country club swimming pools.

He had no notion of the sun's power to dry a baby's diapers,
      turn a working man's neck to leather,
          brighten a lonely old woman's day,
    transform a seed into a summer's worth of pole beans.

If he comes again to the street of clothes lines and pole beans,
      perhaps he will learn about the sun,
and about stars that sparkle brighter than cut glass chandeliers.
Perhaps he will learn the ways of neighbors
whose houses stand almost touching,
      and he will share their wealth.
      Claire Martindale

Sun on a clothesline near Bridgewater, Virginia.
Courtesy Claire Martindale

GOOD FRIDAY, 2020

As I reached to leave the meeting,
the images grew sharper, deeper.
On the screen were windowpanes
of hopeful and resolute people—
friends, teachers—sharing burdens of
dreams deferred and students in need
of love and food and understanding.
In parting, there were cherished words,
warm and real, of pending retirement
and the need for a celebration online.
"I'll drink alone if I have to," I said,
and laughter crossed the frames as
a voice added, "It will be memorable."
It will, indeed.

Later came a pastor's timeless plea:
"Hold on to Good Friday," she urged.
"There is no need to rush Easter—
especially this year—so wait. Wait."
Assurances echoed deep within my
sequestered self and restless soul.
The Resurrection, in all its layers
and all its glory, will soon be here.
It will, indeed.

Quietly, reverently, I lean forward
to darken the candle and wait.

Dan K. Utley

THE GIFT REVISITED

I thought I had a gift, a spiritual one like
you hear about in Adam Hamilton series,
so I shared it with friends to mixed reviews:
"Yep," "Nope," "Not sure," "Close call."
"Could just be a premonition, you know."

Given my age and continuing doubt, I took
it to the "Antiques Roadshow" in Topeka.
"These were quite common in the 1950s,
especially during the Eisenhower years,
but the bottom fell out after Woodstock,
and you rarely see them intact anymore.
Lots of fakes, though, so it's hard to tell.
Could just be a premonition, you know.
By the way, has it ever been refinished?"

Chuck, bless his heart, was supportive,
but his idea of a gift is an inside straight.
Probably best I keep it hidden for now in
a cigar box, like a Dutch Masters I have
in the hall closet under the small Afghan
Grandma Prater knitted when I was born.
Too much public exposure or too many
viewings by slip-sliding confidants and
it might end up as part of a sermon series,
"Common Misconceptions of Stewardship."

The shelf life of gifts is impressive, though,
as they are governed by rules of nature and
cannot be created or destroyed, although
they often suffer a great deal from neglect.
Ultimately, if I choose not to use the gift,
it will go up for auction at my estate sale,
where the transference of ownership will
be clouded by doubt and conjecture, but
will likely pale in lasting value to the box.

Dan K. Utley

BURDEN

She doesn't remember
if anyone spoke the instructions,
or if she was born knowing
that everyone else's happiness
depended on her.

She does recall some
lessons in technique.
How to smile through anger.
How to swallow argument.
How to appear gracious
when she felt like screaming.
The art of little lies,
subtle and effortless,
smoothing every situation.

She watched an older woman, sweet
as a creamy magnolia blossom,
orchestrate the conversation,
making sure her words
softened any turmoil.

Now she's become a master.
She will make you think
her words are what you want
to hear, and her smile
will appear sincere.

Claire Martindale

LISTENING

There are rhythms at a canyon rim
that becalm a searcher's soul,
yet stir it in undiscovered ways
embraced with uncertainty.

I heard them at the Grand watching
daylight fade, stilled in quiet awe
and fretful fear of the route down to
Phantom Ranch I walked at sunrise.

I felt them at the Palo Duro, sitting
with legs off the ledge and eating
at daybreak as windblown crows
circled out just beyond my reach.

In Colorado, I drank them deeply in
as my love and I breathed together
the evening ribbon of the Gunnison
in cold craggy depths of the Black.

I left each rim with echoing rhythms
on my own accord with time to spare,
but now I scan a canyon landscape
of imperfect purple, wondering deep.

Am I not alone? Faint familiar voices,
now blurred by muffled reason and
crimson echoes, linger sad and heavy,
yet fade across the tightening haze.

I did not seek this chasm nor hike the
common trail with signs along the way,
yet this is where I am, assured, dared
by new sounds and restful at the rim.

Dan K. Utley

"LOVEworks" sign promotes Virginia tourism in Dayton, Virginia.
Courtesy Claire Martindale

MERWIN'S "WITNESS"

"I want to tell what the forests were like...."

As the poet wrote, a forest's history
must be told in a forgotten language.
The wild and natural, now cultural,
managed, sustained, or overlooked,
resonant with prevailing mindsets
of the reimagined primal woods.

Wilderness in pure concept yields
to a new canvas, framed anew,
and we mark the vistas, measuring
space through limiting lifetimes.

Yet, just inside the lines we rest,
baptized with airs and sounds the
ancients knew and conveyed with
lost words innately resurrected by
those who choose to witness in
incremental time.

Dan K. Utley

PASSAGE

Before he slammed the door
of the U-Haul and drove
her furniture across four states,
they traversed a thousand miles
in the territory of newfound love.

Before he cleared out drawers
and added shelves to the closet,
he made space in his heart
for her own jig-sawed heart to fit.

Before she posted yard
sale signs and cleaned out
the garage, she discarded
a mantle of lonely yearnings.

Like cartographers drawing maps
of land never trod, together
they charted the boundaries
and staked a homestead
for dreams combined.

Claire Martindale

TO THE DANCER

When she danced, she moved elegantly
        with power and grace,
        and covered every part of the stage.
Those were the signatures of her choreography.

She was forever young, even when she was not,
        a gently gliding spirit on earth,
        seemingly unfettered by limitations.
And yet, all too quickly she was gone,
        and the stage grew dark.
We would be lost if not for memories.

We somehow knew that God danced through her.
        It was spirituality embraced without question,
igniting joyous trailing lights that bounced
        through countless eyes and hearts,
when we were all together many years ago.

The lessons of the dance and the dancer remain
        and float through our minds
        like elusive shadows of a graceful soul
moving in silence across a darkened hall.

In her honor we must listen and love,
        and move with power and grace,
                as best we can,
        dancing together once again in her light,
and using every part of the stage.

                Dan K. Utley

Porcelain portrait on the tombstone of Linda Pate Elrod, Magnolia Cemetery,
Woodville, Texas. *Photo courtesy of Michael Roberts and Tillman Johnson.*

IV. REFLECTIONS FROM WITHIN

Descending dove stained glass window, Bridgewater Church of the Brethren, Bridgewater, Virginia. *Photo courtesy Claire Martindale.*

STIRRING

Gabe bounced out of Sunday School
wearing the craft of the day—a strip
of paper encircling his head. Instead
of feathers he'd stuck jagged red paper cutouts
along the front with a stubby glue stick.
Tongues of fire for Pentecost Sunday.

I envied the little boy.
I wanted a paper headdress to wear,
my own tongues of fire, like the disciples,
to signify the holy touch of God's Spirit.

It was the birth of Christ's church, they say.
Flickering flames blown in by a violent wind
then separating to rest above the followers' heads.
Unschooled in any but their own Galilean
dialect, Jesus' friends began to speak
the tongue of each person in the crowd.
Over a dozen languages, Luke counted.

Like a favorite cap identifying my team,
I want something to show whom I follow,
to proclaim my own encounter
with the Holy Spirit of God.

I sat during worship that morning studying
the stained glass above the choir.
There a dove lowers its head, plunging
toward us with fiery red shards on either side.

I've never glimpsed flames above the heads
of other followers. Never seen the dove sitting
atop their shoulders, murmuring.
Is it because the Spirit moves like wind,
invisible to our eyes?
What I have seen is where the spirit-wind
has been, seen the marks it left,
encountered people whose lives were blown
into order by that holy zephyr.
Can I dare hope that others see
the wind-blown parts of me?

Instead of wearing paper cutouts
I'll watch the clouds sail
and kite tails dance and trees
rustle, seeing where the God
of fire and wind stirs,
working miracles today.

Claire Martindale

UNCERTAIN WORDS

In the time of pandemic
I am at a loss for words in a world
engulfed in uncertainty,
and so I sit and write to make sense
of a senseless time.
If there is purpose in that, it eludes me
in the early morning dark
with a stark, uneasy page.
Perhaps with sunrise,
or a view from the window.
I have little else to do but wait,
or retrace the well-worn trails
around my house.

Dan K. Utley

THE CALLING

How do you know when you receive a call from God?
For me, it started as a nudge, an indistinct interest in a new
group helping people get housing in a creative way. Helping
people help themselves, really. That's what first stirred me.
I told my friends, "I'd like to be part of that one day."

Three years later, the nudge was stronger, and in the mail
a fundraising letter urged: "Is it time for *you* to get
more involved?" Was it, I wondered? I was single but still
had to work for a living. Did getting more involved mean
a full-time change? Mean moving halfway across the country?

A decade before, I experienced the spirit-birth some people call
born again, so I recognized ways of knowing the unknowable—
soul-knowing instead of mind-wisdom. This calling was like
that earlier experience—hearing a voice that can't be heard.

But mind-wisdom has its place. So I traveled halfway
across the country to visit the group's headquarters.
There I was stirred even more by the prospect of using
my faith as part of my work everyday. Still I remained
indecisive until a new friend invited me to come try it
for a while. Why not? It made sense to heart and mind.

Trying it for a while meant making the leap with a safety net. I left my job but held onto to Plan B for my return. I kept the lease on my apartment. Then I got out of my own way and moved for three months. Dipping my toe in the water proved so rewarding that three months turned into six months, and then I dropped Plan B, emptied my apartment and made the move.

I worked as a fulltime volunteer, sharing housing with other volunteers. I met people from faith groups I never knew existed. Not just Catholics, Methodists, Presbyterians, and Baptists, but Mennonites, Hutterites, Brethren and Bruderhof. I met Australian Pentecostals and Evangelicals from Guatemala. We worked together helping people help themselves.

With that perspective, I could see my comfort zone from the outside and found that beyond those once comfortable boundaries were new possibilities. Could I have done and seen and met such people from inside my old limits? Perhaps someone else would have, but I could not.

From that threshold, I knew the calling was true—that I was where I was meant to be. I answered the call because I wanted to change people's lives, and I did. But I know beyond a doubt that the life most changed was my own.

Claire Martindale

BREAD OF HEAVEN

It was suppertime when I drove her home. I was a Big Sister
and she was my Little, and we'd spent the afternoon at the library
in that small southern town. We found her grandmother spooning
food from steaming pots on the stove, and she handed me a plate
to take home for my own meal. A turkey neck, collard greens,
pinto beans, and a thick slab of cornbread. Despite the years I lived
in the south, I never learned to like collards. As for the turkey neck,
I'd never seen one, much less picked the meager meat off the scrawny
bone. But gratitude for the gift meant sharing the same sustenance as the giver.
"God, bless this food," I prayed, "and the hands that prepared it."

My doorbell rang, and there stood a woman I'd met at a storefront church
I attended out of curiosity. Her arms were filled with items wrapped
in freezer paper. "God told me to bring you this meat," she said,
as she carried everything into the kitchen. I pondered the ways
of God and whether The Almighty really directed that offering of pork
chops, chuck roast, and hamburger patties. Then I remembered my next door
neighbors, young men on a volunteer assignment who repaired dilapidated
dwellings for low-income families. Their food stipends ran low this time
of the month. The next day I invited them over for pot roast with potatoes.
"God, bless this food," I prayed, "and the friend you guided to deliver it."

It had been a long day, and the last thing we expected was to see
that parcel near the front door. My husband and I had gone to a doctor
in a nearby city for tests and news of the results. When at last we turned
into our driveway, we were tired in body and drained in spirit. But
then we spied the insulated bag, left by a friend from church.
Inside, protected from summer heat, was a homemade lemon pie,
topped high with meringue, as beautiful as anything on the cover
of a food magazine. Our spirits revived before we took the first bite.
"God, bless this food," I prayed, "and the friend who fed us body and soul."

Claire Martindale

THE LINE

There is a line out there,
invisible, yet somehow indelible,
and I have crossed it far too often
without consequence or concern
as my silence soars above
and troubles the muted self.
Still, the line remains,
deeply incised,
unaltered,
unseen.

Ignored by thoughtless words
or a simple turn of the head,
it trips and tangles and blocks,
yet hews tight to the solid base.
Careful cautions dart about like
wind-borne whispered words.
Only the heart tightens the eye
to sense the line for what it is—
invisible, yet somehow indelible,
often broken, but not beyond repair.

Dan K. Utley

A STAR FOR THE JOURNEY

In the high arc of a Christmas sky, the shimmering stars
      seem to sparkle more brilliantly,
          exquisite jewels that pierce the brittle cold of the
             winter night
      and adorn bare-fingered trees.

Or do they only appear brighter, larger because we search
          the horizon
      for the blazing diamond that
      heralded the long-expected king?

We yearn to see it just as they did—the ragged shepherds,
      the ancient scholars, who followed it to the
          stable yard.
We long for a vision of the Bethlehem star.
We seek to claim its guidance for our journey.
We long for its light to announce again the Messiah—
      the peasant child who was born a king.

Lift your eyes once more.
Stop and look until you really see.
For the star of grace still shines,
      rekindled whenever someone dares to believe
      the Christmas miracle.
Eternally it proclaims the birth of Emmanuel—
      not in the manger of a starlit stable,
      but in the loving cradle of our hearts.

Claire Martindale

THE SHEPHERDS VISIT

The tall man placed another stick on the fire.
A small blaze in a cleared spot on the stable's dirt floor,
     it gave enough light for me to see the weariness in his face.
He said they were from Nazareth,
     and Jonas seemed surprised—
          as if that made our coming here even more improbable.
Jonas was telling the man about the messenger,
     about the heavenly beings who filled the horizon,
          about leaving our flock to come here as we were bid.
We wondered at finding ourselves the only visitors
     to this Bethlehem stable.
Surely there were others who saw the midnight sky ablaze,
     who heard the symphony of angels.
Yet we were alone in attendance to this royal infant.

The babe was fast asleep, wrapped in strips of cloth
     and cushioned in a nest of straw.
He didn't look like a Savior.
But as his mother stroked his tiny head, I could see that she believed he was.
She appeared tired, too, yet her face grew content when Jonas finished his tale,
     as if the telling confirmed something she knew.

The flames began to warm me a bit,
     or something in her eyes,
          or something in the air.
I thought of Moses
     —of what he did when he found God upon the mountain—
          and I knelt to take off my sandals.
Like him, I stood on holy ground.
               Claire Martindale

IN THE HEART OF GOD

Is the space between the beats
infinite or measured?
Is there room enough for dreams
shared and singular?
What of the whispers in the silence?
What of the visions beyond the veil?
Should we linger or should we lead?
Are we who dance in shadowless echoes,
infinite or measured?
Do we dare to know?
Can we dare to know,
in the space between the beats?
Dan K. Utley

THE CHRISTMAS PAGEANT

The buzz of children's whispers
breaks the silence.

A vanguard of angels with pipe-cleaner halos
descends the aisle proclaiming the good news heralded
by celestial beings 20 centuries ago.

Striped dishtowels transform seven-year-olds into
shepherds,
and eight-year-old magi carried bejeweled containers
rescued from garbage pails.

Slowly the procession approaches a cardboard cradle.
Catching the spotlight, a glittering star
swings above the swaddled doll.

Innocently
the children bid us enter their world
of make-believe,
bid us follow them in imagination
to the birthplace of a King,
invite us to suspend
logic

and discover the Lord of the universe in a newborn babe,
encountering with
child-like faith
the Truth that will set us free.
Claire Martindale

A DRAMA UNREHEARSED

Sometimes death comes slowly.
Slowly enough to stage its own private drama.
The players who keep watch must compose their own lines,
       struggling to make familiar words fit an unfamiliar occasion.
Mostly they are silent in the hours of vigil
       when the stage directions call only for waiting.
Silently they sift through memories and wonder what lies beyond,
       straining for a glimpse in the face of the dying.

In the last act, the play changes
       from a deathwatch to a birth wait,
and the watchers, like a mid-wife, prepare to partake of a miracle.
But instead of listening for the newborn's first cry,
they watch in anticipation for the last breath.
When it comes, the observers at the deathbed witness a great mystery
       as visible life becomes invisible.

Here the dialogue fails them altogether.
How can words express the crushing sadness,
the almost guilty relief,
and, to their great surprise,
       the strange disappointment of being left behind?

Claire Martindale

EPILOGUE

The coda for our work is clear—take the time to share your thoughts with a friend, whether through a poem, a song, a dance, a note, a phone or Zoom call, or countless other ways. Each one is a marker, and there's always room for more markers along the way.

ACKNOWLEDGMENTS

First and foremost, I want to acknowledge the encouragement of five remarkable women, each of whom helped me realize that my poetry might be worthy of sharing with others. The first two, Debby Davis Utley and Jane Utley, are duly noted on the dedication page. Both taught me through their abiding and gracious love, that my words mattered to them, and through that revelation I kept expressing myself as best I could to those who also took the time to listen and contemplate. Jane left the stage far too early, but her spirit of overcoming barriers continues to influence others through a special scholarship established in her name at her alma mater, the University of Mary Hardin-Baylor. The third woman worthy of recognition is my co-author, Claire Martindale, who, in the late fall of 1979, hired me to write historical markers for the State of Texas, setting me on a career path in the field of public history. I cannot imagine how my story would have evolved without that first step. Her mentorship and her friendship have blessed me now for more than forty years.

More recently, two other exceptional women helped me—without knowing it at the time, I feel certain—to understand my words had worth far beyond my files and spiral notebooks. At a committee meeting in the fellowship hall of Round Rock Presbyterian Church in 2019, I somehow found enough courage to read one of my spiritual poems (included in this collection as "In the Heart of God") to my friends and fellow committee members, Dr. Haydee Rodriguez and the Rev. Kim Smith-Stanley. The sincerity of their positive and affirming reactions caught me off guard, but in a good way. I know them to be forthright individuals of extraordinary spiritual integrity, so their kind words helped ground my writing and consider partnering with my writer friend, Claire, on this project.

And finally, I want to acknowledge the support and encouragement of two high school friends from Kirby High School in Woodville: Mike Roberts and Linda Pate Elrod. As we sat reminiscing in the early morning hours in the lobby of the Dogwood Motel following a class reunion decades ago, the topic turned somehow to spiritual gifts. Mike is renowned as a singer, building on early local success in rock and roll, and Linda was a successful dance instructor following years of rigorous training and performances. Feeling pride in what each had accomplished, I openly recognized the power of their God-given gifts: Linda for dance and Mike for music. And without missing a beat, Mike said, "And you for writing." It was a life-changing moment that still informs my efforts. Years later—again far too soon—Mike played the guitar and sang at Linda's funeral, and I delivered the eulogy, while our friend danced in heaven. Mike and Linda, Haydee and Kim, and Claire, Debby, and Jane—and many others too numerous to name—can be found among the words I spread across the pages of this book. Those who know me will also hopefully learn to know them as well.

Dan K. Utley

In the depths of the COVID pandemic, here came a call from my friend Dan K. Utley with a bold idea to give meaning to the days of quarantine and confusion. We had been sharing our own poetry with each other for some time, but now Dan suggested that we explore putting together a collection and seeking a publisher. That unleashed a flurry of writing and rewriting as I dug out scribbled drafts and pondered new topics to see how poetic descriptions might illuminate them.

Delving into old files, I thankfully remembered the informal groups of poets I've met with over the years, the contests entered, and the critics who helped me sharpen many pieces. My husband, Steve, has always provided insightful comments and suggestions. I am also grateful to my alma mater, Texas Christian University, for its alumni poetry contest, to which I submitted numerous entries before "Solstice" received the Margie B. Boswell Poetry Award in 2011.

Thanks to Loft Press, Inc. of Fort Valley, Virginia, for including "A Drama Unrehearsed" in the 1996 collection Poetry from the Valley of Virginia. In 2003, "Ranch Road" was printed in the Charlottesville Writing Center's journal Streetlight.

Dan's discernment became invaluable, as he viewed my writing with a poet's eye. He generously shared his experience as a published author of numerous works of history to teach this neophyte the steps toward submission of a promising book.

I am grateful, too, for the people and events that inspired these poems and for those who shared my own journey. With their help, I have found the road rich with stories that can best be told with words that dance across lines of poetry.

Claire Martindale

ABOUT THE AUTHORS

East Texas native Dan K. Utley recently retired as Chief Historian of the Center for Texas Public History at Texas State University. He holds degrees in history from the University of Texas at Austin and Sam Houston State University. The author or editor of numerous books and articles on Texas history, he is a Fellow of the Texas State Historical Association and the East Texas Historical Association, and recipient of the Thomas L. Charlton Award for Lifetime Achievement in Oral History.

Born in Fort Worth, Claire (Williams) Martindale earned degrees in history from Texas Christian University and the University of Arizona at Tucson. She worked on the staff of the Texas Historical Commission from 1974 to 1982, serving as Director of Research. In 1983, she began her career with Habitat for Humanity in Georgia and later in Virginia, where she lives with her husband Steve.